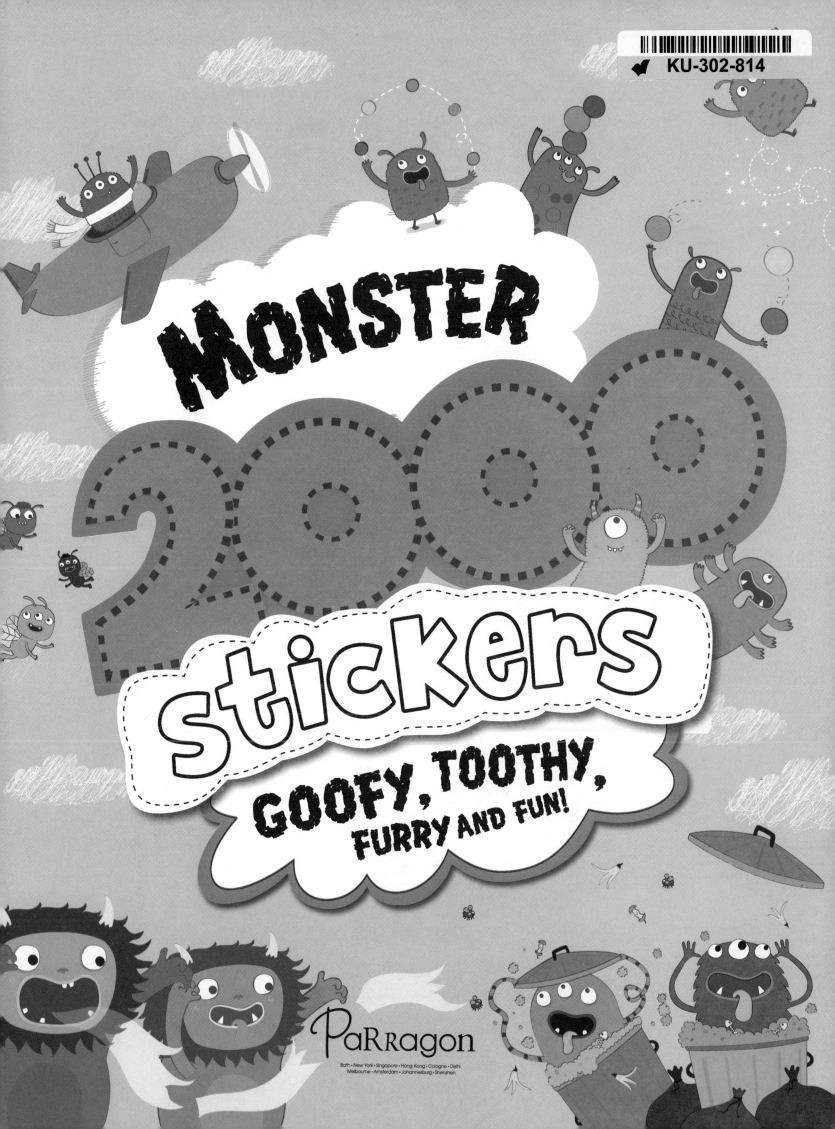

MONSTER
2000
stickers
GOOFY, TOOTHY, FURRY AND FUN!

PaRragon

Bath · New York · Singapore · Hong Kong · Cologne · Delhi
Melbourne · Amsterdam · Johannesburg · Shenzhen

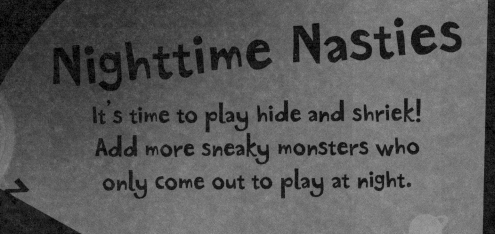

Terrifying Totals

How many monsters have one eye?

How many monsters are drooling?

How many monsters have stripes?

On your marks... Get set... Go!

Spot and circle four differences between these two pictures.

Beasts on the Beach

Even monsters need a break from making mischief.
Add more hairy holidaymakers on the beach!

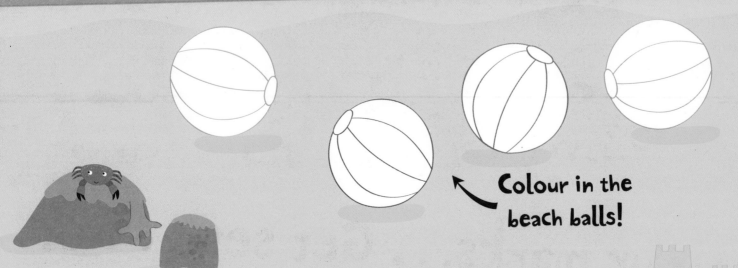

Colour in the
beach balls!

Sun, sand and
sea make me as
happy as can be!

Use your stickers to help the monsters build sandcastles!

Fact File Cards
Count and fill in the missing facts!

Name:

Fluffaluffagus

Eyes: 2

Legs: 2

Grossest fact:

Sneezes snow.

Name:

Three-eyed Yellow Fellow

Eyes:

Legs:

Grossest fact:

Plays with mud.

Name:

Spotto-dotto-saurus

Eyes:

Legs:

Grossest fact:

Sings in the sewers.

Name:

Furbo

Eyes:

Legs:

Grossest fact:

Eats dirty socks.

Scary Scribbles

Scribble some monster bodies.

Make me tall and twisty!

Make me round and wriggly!

Make me long and loopy!

Deep Dark Cave

What creepy creatures are lurking in this cave?
Add more mice, bats and monsters.

No one enters the cave without paying the cave monster!

Use your stickers to give him some gold.

Fuzzy Family!

This monster mum sure has her paws full!

How many crawly critters can you count?

I'm hungry!

I'm sleepy!

Who's Next?

Who comes next in the row – a green bogey beastie or a blue blob monster? Draw its picture in the box.

Shadow Shifters

These monsters are so scary that even their shadows have run away! Help each monster catch its shadow. Draw lines to connect each pair.

A

B

C

D

E

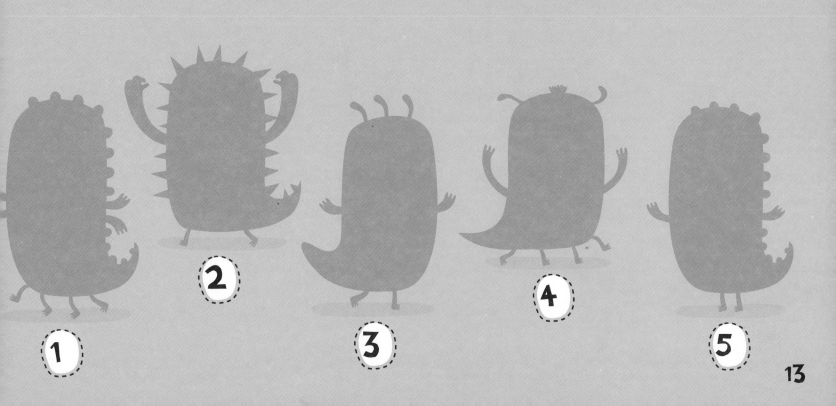

1

2

3

4

5

Monster Party

These furry fun-lovers know how to have a good time!
Fill the room with more monsters and gifts
to help get the party started.

Great party!

Fangs very much!

CAKE CORNER

Colour in these yummy treats!

Pet Hunt

This little girl wants a fuzzy monster for a pet, but these monsters don't want to be tamed! Follow the tangled lines to find out who she catches.

Come back!

Which cuddly critter will become this little girl's pet?

Monsterrific Motors

Spot and circle five differences between these two pictures, before they drive away!

Monster Trucks

Vroom vroom! These monsters won't get far without wheels.

Draw some giant tyres so that the trucks can crush cars and flatten fences as the monsters crash their way to the finish line.

Outta my way!

Underwater Uglies

Glug glug. Fill this watery world with more sea monsters.
Don't forget their fishy friends!

Mystery Monster

What does this monster look like? Connect the dots to find out.

Colour me in too!

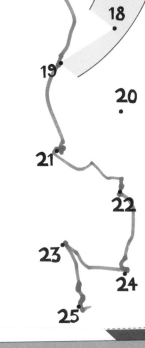

Next, Please! Who's next in the queue?
Draw a picture of the missing monster in each row.

Dream Drawing

After a long, hard day of monster mischief, this sleepyhead
is taking a nap. But what is he dreaming about?

Grubby Garden

It's time to take the bins out – but beware of the bin beasties!
Fill the bins with more stinky monsters and yucky rubbish.

Eeek!

23

Buzz Off!

Colour in each bug beastie's matching friend in the same colours.

Then draw lines to join us with our matching friends!

Monster Mix

Monsters come in all shapes and sizes!

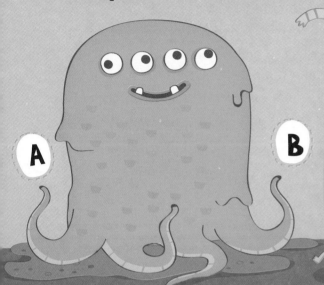

Which monster is the tallest?

Which monster is the shortest?

Which monster is the fattest?

Which monster is the thinnest?

A

B

C

D

Fearsome Faces!

Decorate these monster shapes with l...
a...

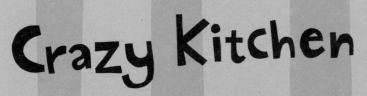

Crazy Kitchen

These mischievous monsters have taken over
the kitchen and made an awful mess!
Add more tiny troublemakers.

Paint Puddles!

These monsters are made of gloopy globs of paint!
Colour them in with the colour that
matches their paint puddle.

Monster on the Loose

Spot and circle four differences between these two pictures.

Frost Bite!

B-b-b-b-brrrrrr!
Add more sledging, skating and
snowball-fighting monsters!

Wheee!

Draw Your Own Yeti!

1 Draw a round body, two legs and two feet.

2 Add the head, two arms and paws with sharp claws.

3 Now draw some fur to help keep your yeti warm!

Monster Munchies

Which lucky monster will reach the delicious bowl of wormlicious spaghetti?

A

B

C

I'm starving!

Creepy Colour Corner

From scruffy and green to tidy and clean!
Give this thumbprint monster a new crazy hair colour and style in the mirror.

What is floating in the tank? Draw something yucky!

Frightening Fangs!

Draw some scary monster faces to go with these terrifying teeth.

Monster Match

Match each mummy monster with her baby beastie.

 **A**

 **B**

 **C**

 **D**

1

2

3

4

Monster Dance Off

Circle the odd one out in each
team of dangerous dancers.
Then give each monster
dance group a name.

HIP-HOP HAIRBALLS

Horrible Hill

It's a dark and stormy night in the fearsome forest!
Add grizzly monsters in the graveyard
and bats zooming around the sky.

Add more bones
for the monsters
to munch on!

Dotty Drawing

Connect the dots to find out what is missing from this monster's head.

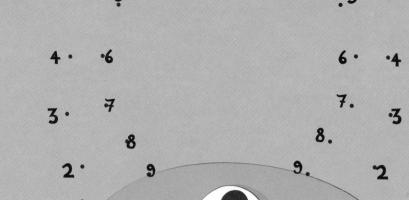

Monstertastic Masterpiece

Use crazy colours to brighten up this bunch of monsters.

40

Look Before You Leap!

How many tickle monsters are hiding in the ball pool?

Slimy Swamp Swimming

Make a splash and fill this
gloopy green swamp with monsters!

Where did the frog go after he was bitten by a monster?

The HOPspital!

43

Misfit Monsters

Circle the odd monster out in each row.

Draw Your Own Two-horned Glob Monster!

1

2

3

First, draw a gross glob.

Add some horrible horns.

Finally, draw the face. Grrr!

44

Meet the Space Monsters!

Space monsters from Planet Goo are visiting
their friends on the Gooey Green Moon!

Wheeee!

Add more monsters and some toys for them to play with.

Answers

Page 4

Page 5

3 monsters have one eye.
2 monsters are drooling.
2 monsters have stripes.

Page 8

Yellow monster: **3** eyes, **7** legs
Orange monster: **2** eyes, **4** legs
Green monster: **1** eye, **8** legs

Page 12

There are **5** crawly critters.

Page 13

A3, B1, C2, D5, E4

Page 16

Monster **C** will become the little girl's pet.

Page 20

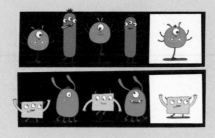

Page 24

A4, B3, C1, D2

Page 25

Monster **B** is the tallest.
Monster **C** is the shortest.
Monster **A** is the fattest.
Monster **D** is the thinnest.

Page 28

A4, B5, C2, D3, E1

Page 29

Page 32

Monster A will have the wormlicious spaghetti.

Page 36

A3, B4, C2, D1

Page 37

Page 40

Page 41

There are **6** tickle monsters hiding in the ball pool.

Page 44